nature
crafts

LANDAUER BOOKS

nature
crafts

Copyright© 2006 by Landauer Corporation

This book was designed, produced, and published by Landauer Books
A division of Landauer Corporation
3100 NW 101st Street, Urbandale, IA 50322
www.landauercorp.com

President/Publisher: Jeramy Lanigan Landauer
Director of Operations: Kitty Jacobson
Editor in Chief: Becky Johnston
Managing Editor: Jeri Simon
Art Director: Laurel Albright
Project Designers: Laurel Albright, Linda Bender, Kitty Jacobson,
Brooke Johnston, Margaret Sindelar, Sue Voegtlin
Contributing Writer: Connie McCall
Technical Writer: Rhonda Matus
Technical Illustrator: Linda Bender
Editorial Assistants: Debby Burgraff, Judy Hunsicker
Photographer: Craig Anderson Photography

Library of Congress Cataloging-in-Publication Data
Easy does it nature crafts : 60 seasonal projects for quick gifts and home décor.
  p. cm.
 ISBN-13: 978-1-890621-42-1 (alk. paper)
 ISBN-10: 1-890621-42-0 (alk. paper)
 1. Nature craft. I. Title: Nature crafts.
TT157.E287 2006
745.5--dc22

2006045232

This book printed on acid-free paper.
Printed in China

10-9-8-7-6-5-4-3-2-1

ISBN 13: 978-1-890621-42-1
ISBN 10:   1-890621-42-0

Introduction

Celebrate the seasons with a wealth of unique inspirations to make for home and table decorations as well as gifts and greetings featured in this 112-page crafting treasury. Choose from popular crafting techniques including beading, decoupage, sponge-painting, stamping, flower arranging and wreath making to create 60 projects inspired by nature's beauty.

Discover how easy it is to use fresh, dried, or silk flowers, fruit, gourds, greenery and natural treasures—from the seashore to the woodlands—for dozens of wall décor, centerpieces or tabletop displays.

Start by reading through Basics that shows you how to get simple tools and supplies organized—many of which you'll likely already have on hand. Then refer to special topics about crafting techniques to help you:

- Learn how to preserve fresh flowers through pressing or drying

- Create one-of-a-kind invitations, gift wraps and greetings

- Store your memories from the seashore in a keepsake box

- Perk up a party with natural favors for guests to take home

- Have fun with feathers added to wreaths and centerpieces

- Gather up gourds and greens for almost instant decorating

For easy reference, each project is shown in full color with complete materials list and step-by-step illustrated instructions.

Best of all, there's something fun for everyone—even families on the go. Scattered throughout the book you'll find one-hour crafts that are truly a fast faux finish. Enjoy!

Becky Johnston
Editor in Chief

CONTENTS

basics

spring

summer

CONTENTS

autumn

winter

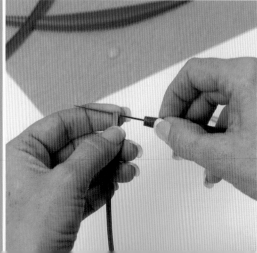

basics

getting *started*

essential tools for nature crafts

You probably own most of the tools and supplies that are called for in the "Gather" section of each project. These common household items all are used in one or more of the projects:

Scissors and Blades

1. **Comfort-Grip Shears** are comfortable and lightweight. These shears are designed to allow fabric or paper to be cut as it lies on a flat work surface.

2. **Decorative Edging Scissors** feature shaped blades to create decorative edges on paper. Pinking shears may also be used.

3. **Small Scissors** are ideal for small cutting details or clipping threads.

4. **Craft knife** has a thin handle and a sharp, pointed blade that offers precision in detail cutting. A variety of blades are available.

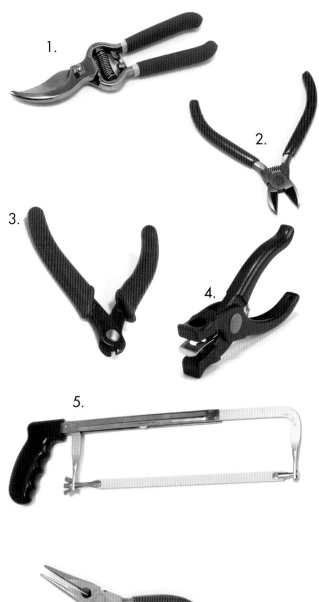

Cutters

1. Gardening Shears often feature a spring-action handle with a notch in the blades for clipping wires.

2. Wire Cutters have short, straight blades that easily cut through wire.

3. Wire Snippers cut cleanly through wire to leave a safe, straight edge.

4. Hole Punch now comes in a variety of circle sizes from 1/16" to 1/4" and in interesting shapes such as hearts, diamonds and rectangles.

5. Small Hand Saw is helpful in cutting fresh greenery.

Pliers

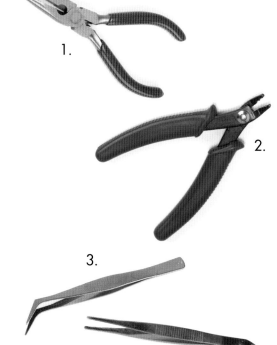

1. Needle Nose Pliers are commonly used when working with silk or fresh flowers and greenery. They are also used for beadwork and wire crafts.

2. Crimping Pliers are designed to crimp spacer beads when jewelry-making. They help to eliminate any sharp edges that may occur when cutting beads or wiring.

3. Tweezers are ideal for picking up beads or arranging small embellishments and stickers. They are also the perfect tool for holding items in place while gluing.

Tapes and Glues

1. **Floral Tape** is self-adhering, so it must be wrapped tightly in overlapping layers to adhere.

2. **Strapping Tape** is strong enough for heavy-duty taping.

3. **Craft Glue** dries clear and can be used on a variety of surfaces—from paper and fabric to wood and leather.

4. **Spray Adhesive** is excellent for temporary bonding and allows for repositioning. It bonds most acetate, foils, fabrics, light tissues and newsprint.

5. **Glue Sticks** are used in a glue gun (see opposite page).

Wires

1. **Floral Wire** may be purchased in precut lengths or on a spool. It is most often used for attaching accents or greenery to a wreath.

2. **Copper Wire** is a thin, strong wire used for floral decorations.

3. **Beading Wire** is strong and pliable for stringing beads and charms.

Miscellaneous

- Drill
- Sandpaper
- 1" Sponge Brush
- Small Flat-tip Paintbrush
- Artist's Paintbrushes
- Fine-tip Black Marking Pen
- Clear Acrylic Varnish
- Food Coloring
- Quilling Tool

primary tool for nature crafts

For many of the projects, you will need a glue gun. Both low-temperature and hot glues work on almost any surface and come in many varieties, including colored glue, white for caulking, and glue with metallic glitter.

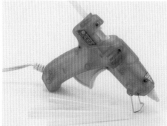

Glue Gun Safety Precautions

• Wear clothing that glue will not penetrate; use eye protection. Before plugging in a glue gun, set a steady container of ice water within easy reach.

• Using a power strip with a breaker is recommended. Avoid extension cords if possible.

• Remain alert and keep the hot glue gun out of the reach of chidren. Always unplug the gun and put it in a safe place if you need to walk away from the work area.

About a Glue Gun

A hot glue gun melts glue at about 350 degrees; be very careful not to burn your hands. A warm glue gun is safer, but does not heat at such high temperatures. While there is no difference in the actual bonding of either glues, a warm glue gun may not be as effective in certain projects due to its lower heat setting.

Newer types of glue guns are dual-heat, which can be used as either hot glue or warm glue;

cordless, which retains heat for a few minutes after being unplugged; and ColdHeat™, which uses a battery for instant melting and has a tip protector.

Choosing a Glue Gun

When you purchase a glue gun, choose one that fits your hand comfortably. Hot glue and warm glue guns each have "plus" and "minus" factors. Hot glue melts quickly, sets quickly and is not as messy as some other adhesives, but the glue may be runny. The most serious drawback is that careless use could lead to burns.

The greatest "plus" factor for low-temperature glue guns is their safety. Some are even described as "safe for classroom use." You can use low-temperature glues with delicate materials like lace and nylon, but the glue may cool and set too quickly.

Note: Use caution when switching between hot and warm while using a dual-heat glue gun.

To clean a glue gun, cool the gun and rub it completely with a dryer sheet. Tip: Dryer sheets also keep glues and paints from sticking to your hands. Keep extra glue sticks in the freezer to cut down on their tendency to be stringy when they are heated.

To use a glue gun:

1. Plug it in and insert the correct glue stick. Use the trigger to pump the glue stick down into the barrel of the gun, making sure that the glue stick reaches the end of the heated nozzle. If you have a large glue gun, you might need to insert two glue sticks the first time you use it.

2. Let the glue gun heat for about 10 minutes. It must be completely hot so glue flows freely. Do not force glue through the glue gun. While you wait, spread newspapers over your work area to protect it.

3. Before you apply glue, make sure you have materials placed exactly where you want them. To apply glue to a surface, lightly squeeze the trigger. Hold the glued object in place for a minute, or longer if it is large or heavy. If there are strands or strings of dried glue, break them off.

4. If your hand comes in contact with hot glue, quickly dip your hand in cold water and then peel off the hardened glue.

5. Keep the glue gun upright in its built-in stand when not in use. If it does not have a stand, use a plate or a non-flammable substitute.

gathering *naturals*

basic guide to harvesting & arranging

You may have some of the supplies listed in the "Gather" section of each project on hand. The items used are readily available at your local craft or hobby store, or perhaps even in your own backyard.

Using Fresh Flowers

Whether from your garden, fields, or the florist, fresh flowers bring unmatched beauty and fragrance to any project. One drawback is that fresh flowers do not last as long as dried or artificial flowers.

Projects that use fresh flowers work well for a special event or a special season. Depending on the project, flowers can be inserted into wet foam or into a pretty container that is part of a gift. They can also be planted in tiny flowerpots or tucked into water-filled floral tubes.

A floral tube is plastic and shaped like a test tube, but with a narrow slit in the lid for the flower's stem. The base of the tube is pointed and can be inserted into a wreath base or other arrangement.

Use fresh flowers or leaves on wreaths or arrangements to adorn a wedding table, holiday centerpieces, or an anniversary or birthday celebration.

Harvesting Flowers

Flowers that are to be dried using any of the following methods should be picked on a sunny day after the dew has dried. Late morning is often the best time. Choose flowers that are at their peak and with as few flaws as possible. Drying magnifies any flaws such as insect damage.

Pick more than are needed, to allow for inevitable shrinkage. Do not pick more than can be processed in one day. Try to begin the drying process within an hour or two after picking the flowers.

Drying Flowers

There are several methods of drying flowers to preserve them. Some of the most common are pressing, air-drying, drying in the microwave oven and drying with a desiccant. Choice of method depends on the type of flower or other material you are using.

Natural Air-drying

Some flowers are especially suited for a "fresh-into-dried" treatment. Hydrangea is a good example. Placed in 1 or 2 inches of cold water and left in a warm room, the flowers dry as the water evaporates, leaving a naturally dried bloom.

Hydrangea is commonly used in wreaths, so drying these flowers is a good investment. This method also works with everlastings, baby's breath, cornflowers, Chinese lanterns, and honesty (moonflower).

A traditional method of drying flowers is hanging them upside down to dry naturally. Choose a space that is warm, well-ventilated, dry and semi-dark, as direct sunlight will cause the blooms to fade. Hanging the flowers in small bunches fastened with a twistband and hung from

a nail or a clothesline works best for herbs and flowers that have compact blooms. Peony buds, rosebuds, partly opened marigolds, celosia, dusty miller and delphiniums all dry well using this method.

When bundling the flowers, each bundle should have the same kind and size of flower, and be at the same open stage. Pull off some of the less attractive leaves when dried.

Use a screen to dry flowers that spread out flat, like daisies and cosmos. An old window screen propped up on boxes will work well. Insert the stems down through the screen. Enlarge the holes if necessary.

Drying flowers naturally takes anywhere from a week to a month, depending on the flowers and the humidity. During that month they are an attractive natural decoration with a pleasant fragrance.

Microwave Drying

Drying flowers in the microwave is a fairly new method. Since microwaves vary, experiment a bit to see how much time is required to dry different types of flowers. In general, flowers and small sprays of leaves are dry in 3 to 4 minutes.

Arrange the flowers on a paper towel on the microwave's turntable. Place stemmed flowers with stems toward the center but not touching. Start the microwave on full power and check the flowers after 3 minutes. Give them a little more time if they do not feel as crisp as paper. Let them cool a minute before removing them from the oven. Store them in a box lined with tissue paper.

Microwave drying on the turntable without a drying agent works for small composite flowers such as cornflowers or feverfew and for flat open-faced flowers such as pansies. It also works for some leaf sprays.

It does not work, however, for trumpet-shaped flowers like daffodils. This type of flower needs to be used with a desiccant. A desiccant is a drying agent such as borax, kitty litter, sand or silica gel. Silica gel is the preferred choice. It is available in crafts stores and at some garden centers and florist shops and it is reusable.

To dry shaped flowers in the microwave, put a thin layer of silica gel in the bottom of a microwave-safe container.

Arrange flowers in a single layer and cover them with another layer of silica gel. Each surface and petal of the flower should be in contact with the desiccant. Microwave the flowers on medium power for about 2 minutes and allow a standing time of 10 minutes. Check them and if they are not dry, microwave them again at 15 second intervals.

Desiccant Drying

Silica gel, today's preferred floral drying agent, is a sand-like substance with light crystals. Cover flowers in it and it absorbs moisture from them relatively quickly. Drying time is measured

in days, not weeks; typically flowers are dried in 3 to 7 days.

Use airtight containers with only one species of flower at a time. Trim off stems. Place about 1/2" of silica gel in the bottom of the container. For flat-faced flowers like daisies, lay the flowers facedown on the gel. For bell-shaped or spiked flowers, such as snapdragons, lay them on their sides. For flowers with multiple petals, like roses, peonies and marigolds, lay the flowers faceup on the gel.

The flowers should not overlap or touch each other.

Carefully sprinkle the silica gel between petals on each flower, separating the layers a bit. Gently sift more silica gel over the flowers until they are fully covered. Try to keep petals in their natural position and avoid crushing them.

When finished, close container and label with the date and the kind of flower. Store the container where it is dark and dry, but where it will be seen from time to time so the flowers will be checked regularly. Begin checking on the second day. Thin-petalled flowers may be dry by the third day; bulky flowers often take a week.

When the flowers feel crisp and dry, carefully remove the silica gel and use tweezers to gently pull out the dried flowers. Use a soft brush to whisk away any dusty residue.

How to Press Flowers

Ferns, leaves, and some varieties of flowers can be pressed.

Flowers with thin petals, such as pansies, violas, clematis or petunias work best.

A common method most people use when they need to press only a few pansies is to lay the blossoms facedown on a piece of absorbent paper, cover them with a second piece of absorbent paper, and place the "sandwich" between the pages of a large book. A telephone directory works well and will hold three or four layers. Set additional heavy books or objects on top for more weight.

If pressing large quantities of botanical materials, a flower press may be worth the investment. It has a sturdy wooden frame with straps to tighten it and allows several layers to be pressed at once. It also comes with heavy blotting paper and cardboard ventilators.

Assembling a Wreath

When going to a crafts store to buy a wreath base, there are a variety of materials, shapes, and sizes. Select a base that will complement the materials being used.

Foam Bases

Most foam wreath bases are flat on the back, rounded on the front and come in a variety of sizes, shapes and thicknesses. Larger bases are often reinforced with a molded-in metal ring that allows them to hold heavier materials.

Covering a foam base before working on it has two advantages: it helps to avoid little patches of foam showing through the finished wreath, and glue can be used easily. Some glues dissolve foam if they are applied directly, and hot glue may burn into the foam. To cover the base, wind wide ribbon around it, or use sheet moss for a uniform background, color and texture.

Pin the material in place with floral picks, which are small wooden picks with a length of fine-gauge wire attached. If using wide ribbon, choose a color that matches the materials you plan to use.

Plant materials that have sturdy stems can be pushed directly into the foam. Make a small starter hole first. For plant materials that have weaker stems, or no stems at all, use floral picks or a hot glue gun.

There are also "wet-foam" bases that can be soaked in water and used as a base for fresh flowers.

Wire Bases

Flat wire bases may be purchased in two varieties. A single wire wreath is nice to use with light and delicate materials. A double wire can be wrapped with brown paper or colorful ribbon.

Wire bases are also available with several rings of heavy wire, making a three-dimensional base. The arrangement of the rings makes a hollow trench. Attach materials with thin-gauge floral wire or monofilament line, such as fishing line.

Twig & Vine Bases

Grapevine is one of the most popular materials for a wreath base. It is attractive by itself, which makes it a good choice when making a wreath that is not fully covered. A "crescent wreath" that covers only the top or bottom of the base is an example. Twig bases are more rustic looking and less regular in shape since the twigs are not as pliable as grapevine.

To attach materials to a vine or twig base, a hot glue gun or thin wire is generally used. Some flowers can be gathered into a small bunch and wired to a floral pick which is then inserted at an angle along the wreath materials and affixed with a little glue.

Choosing Materials

Fresh, dried or artificial flowers work well in wreaths. Flowers of any kind bring the garden's beauty indoors.

Craft stores carry a huge variety of artificial flowers and greenery. Dried grasses in their natural colors, and in some dyed colors as well, may also be purchased at a craft store.

Several of the projects call for non-floral extras from nature, objects such as feathers, seashells, fruits, berries and stones. Craft stores carry all of these items and more, plus an abundant array of artificial and dried flowers.

Choosing Gourds

The gourd family includes pumpkins, squashes, melons, cucumbers and the brightly colored fruit we call gourds.

Ornamental gourds are inedible. They have thin, hard shells, generally with little flesh inside. Gourds must be thoroughly mature before picking, with stems and tendrils having turned brown. They also must be thoroughly dried before you use them in crafts.

Our *Gourmet Gourds Centerpiece*, page 89, contains an assortment of ornamental gourds. They come in many shapes, and most of them are named for their shape—for example, the spoon, bottle, pear, penguin, kettle and dipper gourds. The pale cream gourd with ten small projections around its top is known as the Crown of Thorns gourd.

Gourds vary in size, from tiny, the *Mini Gourd Candleholders*, at right, to fairly large. The colors that are most familiar are green,

orange, cream and yellow. The skin can be smooth, bumpy or downright knobby.

If a gourd is grown inside a box or a container that is carved on the inside, the mature gourd will have that box shape or container pattern. People around the world use gourds to make musical instruments, spoons, pipes, canteens, birdhouses, bath sponges, decorations and many other things.

Growing Gourds

Gourds have three basic needs: sun, water and well-fertilized soil. They need about four months of frost-free weather and at least six hours of sunshine a day.

Keep in mind that these plants vine and often grow to 30 or 40 feet. They will spread out unless trained to grow up a trellis or fence. A variety of small gourds can be grown in a container, preferably with a circle of fencing tucked into the edge of the container to provide support for the vines. By nature, gourds are climbers and there are advantages to growing them upright.

Soil should be slightly acidic and well-drained. When the soil is about 70 degrees, it is time to plant the seeds or seedlings. Gourds hybridize easily, so what you get from any given seed is unpredictable. Seeds from a commercial seed company usually germinate well and are relatively true to variety. Soaking the seeds for a day or so will help germination, which can take up to two weeks.

After the plants come up, keep the soil moist. If several plants come up, choose the strongest and pull the others so there are only one or two plants in a hill. For a week or so, not much growth will occur above ground as the roots are growing. When the vine is about 10 feet long, cut off the top so the plant will branch. It will bear both male and female blossoms, male on the primary vine and female on the branches.

Gourds need plenty of water, because like most fruits they are 90 percent water. They also have large leaves that cause a lot of water evaporation. Garden plants should have a deep watering at least once a week and container plants more often.

After approximately six weeks, add a well-balanced fertilizer that contains nitrogen. Once baby gourds appear, fertilizing should not include nitrogen. As they grow, watch for insects, especially squash beetles.Dust the plants with an insecticide. Help protect the little gourds by slipping a paper plate or a piece of cardboard under them. Sprinkle the insecticide on the plate.

At the end of the season, do not pick the gourds until the vines and tendrils have withered and turned brown. Store them in a dry place for curing, allowing the moisture to leave the gourd. It will take 3 to 6 months for the gourds to dry enough to hear the seeds rattle. An epidermis may develop as the gourd dries; soak it in warm water for an hour or so, and then gently scrape it off with a dull knife.

pansy *tea box*

Welcome spring with blooms on a box. Place pressed pansy petals under glass and add a dusting of glitter spray to embellish a purchased box just right for tea for two.

 Remove the glass and backboard from the box lid. Using the sponge brush, paint the outside surfaces and lid of the box purple. When the paint is dry, sand lightly and wipe off the dust with a clean cloth. With the sponge brush apply  a light coat of cream to the previously painted surfaces. Let dry. Use sandpaper to distress the box, lightly sanding to remove some of the cream paint and allowing the purple to show through as desired. Wipe with the cloth.

 Thin the craft glue with water. Glue a cutout onto one corner of the lid as shown. Use a flat brush to apply diluted glue to the backs of the desired cutouts. Glue cutouts to the sides of the box and smooth. When the glue is dry, coat the outside surface of the box with the spray enamel.

 Cut scrapbook paper the same size as the backboard. Adhere the paper to the board with spray adhesive. Arrange and mount the pansies on the paper, using a toothpick to apply a dot of craft glue to the back of each flower. Insert the glass and backboard in the lid.

Gather

Wood box with hinged, framed glass lid

Acrylic paint: purple and cream

Sponge brush (1-inch)

Sandpaper

Clean cloth

Paper cutouts

Craft glue

Small flat brush

Clear enamel spray with glitter

Scrapbook paper

Spray adhesive

Pressed pansies

Toothpick

fast faux finish

Pansy Magnet Invite spring into your kitchen by filling a purchased magnetic frame with pressed pansy blooms.

strawberry *melting bowl*

*I*mpress your guests with these simple, yet elegant, strawberry bowls. Fill these creations with cake or fresh berries and cream for a delicious dessert or a tempting treat at teatime.

1 Thaw the frozen strawberries. If using fresh berries, cut them into small pieces, sprinkle with sugar, and refrigerate until berries are syrupy.

2 Divide the berries equally between the two 14-ounce bowls. Place an 8-ounce bowl inside each larger bowl. Press down on the small bowl to force the berries up, filling the space between the bowls without spilling over.

3 Use strapping tape to hold the smaller bowls in place. Cover with plastic wrap and freeze until solid.

4 To remove the plastic bowls, set in warm water for 15 seconds, increasing the time by 5 second intervals as needed to remove the outer bowl. Carefully pour warm water in the small bowl and let set as needed to remove the inner bowl.

5 Keep bowls in the freezer until ready to serve. Fill the bowls with dessert of your choice.

Gather

1 Pint of fresh or frozen strawberries

2—14-ounce and
2—8-ounce plastic bowls

Strapping tape

Plastic wrap

Dessert of your choice, such as shortcake, additional berries, and whip cream or ice cream

citrus
centerpiece

*F*resh flowers combine with lemons and limes for a
unique centerpiece topped with sparkling sugar sprinkles—
a lovely setting for ice-cold lemonade and cookies.

1 Working with one lemon or lime, coat with spray adhesive. Immediately sprinkle generously with sugar sprinkles. Repeat with remaining lemons and limes.

2 Arrange the fruit on the serving dish.

3 Trim the stems of the flowers as needed to achieve the desired length. Insert the flowers between lemons and limes to fill the spaces.

Lemons and limes

Spray adhesive

White sparkling
sugar sprinkles

Serving dish

Fresh flowers of choice

fast faux finish

Recipe Cards Bright card stock complete with a favorite pie recipe and decorated with stickers or beads will let guests know they're welcome anytime.

bamboo
party favor

Create a warm welcome for guests by arranging a bamboo shoot in an elegant container surrounded by river pebbles. The personalized place cards invite guests to take home the special favor to commemorate the event.

1 Insert bamboo stalk into glass container. Hold the stalk upright and fill the area around it with river pebbles. Add water.

Bamboo stalk

Small, clear glass container

River pebbles

Card stock

Scraps of decorative paper

Paper adhesive

Hole punch

Fine-tip black pen

Raffia

2 Cut a small rectangle of card stock. Cut smaller rectangles of decorative paper and layer on the card stock with adhesive, leaving space to personalize. Punch a hole in the top left corner of the card.

3 Write the guest's name on the card. Insert a thread of raffia through the hole and tie the card to the glass container.

fast faux finish

Use a smooth, flat stone tied with a strip of leather to design a *napkin tie* that continues the Asian party theme.

floral
pomander

*P*omander, from Old French *pome d'embre*, or "apple of amber," is an aromatic mixture. Make several of these striking pomander balls to lend a gentle fragrance and a touch of spring to every room in your home.

1 Hot glue pieces of sheet moss onto the plastic foam ball until it is completely covered.

2 To use dried flowers, carefully trim the stems as needed to achieve the desired depth on the ball. Beginning with the largest flowers and progressing to the smallest, individually hot glue the flowers onto the ball. Hold each in place until the glue sets. Continue adding flowers until the ball is completely covered.

3 To use potpourri, apply hot glue to a small area of the ball. Immediately roll the glued area of the ball in the potpourri. Continue this process until the ball is completely covered with potpourri.

4 Place the flower covered ball on a candlestick.

Gather

Plastic foam ball (ours are 4—5-inch-diameter)

Sheet moss

Dried flowers or potpourri

Scissors

Hot glue gun and glue sticks

Candlesticks

Refer to Glue Gun Safety Precautions on page 15 before beginning this project.

fast faux finish

Daisies or other large blooms offer a quick coverup for a styrofoam ball that becomes the perfect focal point for a decorative grouping.

living *wreath*

This rustic wreath shouts Spring with its many symbols of new life—butterflies, bunnies, and live spider plants growing in three terra cotta flowerpots.

Cut pieces of assorted greenery. Visualizing the wreath as a clock face, position greenery at 11 and 2 o'clock, and from 5 to 9 o'clock on the front surface of the wreath. Hot glue the greenery in place.

 Weave the ribbon around the wreath and wire in place. Hot glue or wire the seasonal elements on the greenery. Cut small pieces of flower heads and hot glue these around the seasonal elements. Tuck bead sprays into the wreath and secure with hot glue.

 Using the sponge brush, paint the outside surfaces of the terra cotta pots.

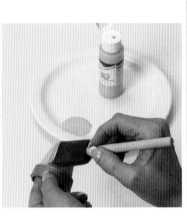

 When the paint is dry, hot glue the pots to the wreath. Use a small amount of potting soil to plant the spider plant starts in the pots.

Gather

Grapevine wreath

Assorted silk greenery and small flowers

Green-and-white check ribbon (3/4-inch-wide)

Florist's wire

Wire cutters

Assorted seasonal elements, such as eggs, bunnies, chicks and butterflies

Hot glue gun and glue sticks

Bead sprays

3 Miniature terra cotta pots

Acrylic paint in desired colors

Sponge brush

Potting soil

Spider plant starts

Refer to Glue Gun Safety Precautions on page 15 before beginning this project.

fast faux finish

Dress up a springtime table with a mixture of colorful jelly beans in a painted terra cotta pot with a ring of daisies tucked in the water tray.

rosebud *hearts*

*L*et your love shine through with these frames that boast flowers and tiny ribbon hearts. Make these thoughtful gifts for special occasions, Mother's Day or wedding anniversaries.

Remove the glass from the frame and place it on the right side of the scrapbook paper, positioning it to include the desired pattern. Draw around the glass shape with a pencil and cut out just inside the pencil line. Insert the paper shape and the backboard in the frame. You will not need the frame glass for this project.

 To make an open heart, fold a quilling or paper strip in half; the fold is the bottom of the heart. Roll each end around a quilling tool or toothpick toward the center of the heart, keeping the strip's edges as even as possible.

 To make a two-piece heart, roll a quilling or paper strip around a quilling tool or toothpick, keeping the edges of the strip even. Slide the coil off the quilling tool and allow the coil to loosen. Use a toothpick to apply a drop of glue on the loose end and press in place. When the glue is dry, shape the coil into a teardrop by pinching one end. Make two teardrops for each heart.

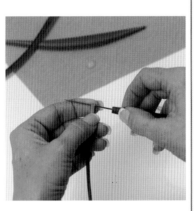

 Use a small amount of glue to attach the quilled hearts on the scrapbook paper shapes, positioning two teardrops side-by-side for the two-piece hearts.

 Trim the stems of the dried flowers to the desired length. Hot glue the larger flowers on the scrapbook paper first and then fill in with smaller flowers.

 # Gather

Heart-shaped silver frame

Variety of scrapbook paper, including word print

Quilling strips or colored paper (1/8-inch-wide)

Quilling tool (optional)

Toothpicks

Clear craft glue

Dried flowers in two sizes

Hot glue gun and glue sticks

Refer to Glue Gun Safety Precautions on page 15 before beginning this project.

fast faux finish

Capture a mother's heart by cutting a heart shape from scrapbook paper, putting it in the frame, and hot gluing a silk rose to the frame.

floral
cake ring

*T*urn any event into a special occasion by dressing up a plain white cake with fresh flowers in bold, dramatic colors. For a bridal shower, use flowers in the bride's colors.

 **1** Trim and clean the stems of the flowers and greens, leaving each slightly longer than you think is necessary. This will allow you to adjust the stem length as needed when designing the arrangement.

 2 Beginning with the main background flower, push the stems into or underneath the cake. If you plan on serving this cake, use flowers that are edible or decorate only the front half and cut pieces from the back.

 3 Evenly space the accent flowers among the background flowers. Add the greens. Fill in any spaces with smaller filler flowers.

4 Make a small bouquet and lay on top of the cake.

Frosted cake

Assorted fresh flowers
and greens

fast faux finish

Color-coordinated ribbons and a few fresh blossoms are a stylish accent for the serving pieces.

garden flowers decoupage

Fruit and floral prints, such as those by New England folk artist Warren Kimble, give a grouping of galvanized steel containers a vintage, antique look when decoupaged with a clear, acrylic varnish.

 Use a sponge brush to apply a coat of black gesso to the outside surfaces of the metal can.

 When the gesso is dry, use a sponge brush to basecoat the can with acrylic paint in the color of your choice. Let the basecoat dry. Lightly sponge on a second color of paint with a sea sponge. Allow the paint to dry thoroughly.

 Thin craft glue with water. Use a sponge brush to apply a smooth coat of diluted glue on the back of the art print. Smooth the art print onto the front of the can.

 When the glue is dry, sponge the edges of the art print with both colors of paint. Let the paint dry.

 Apply several coats of clear acrylic varnish to the can, following the manufacturer's instructions.

Gather

Metal cans of choice

Black gesso

Sponge brushes

Acrylic paints of choice

Sea sponge

Art print

Craft glue

Clear acrylic varnish

summer

gerbera
gift box

Spring into summer with this cheerful painted box filled with daisies. Individual flowers are placed in water-filled vials and wrapped in bright tissue to stay fresh longer.

Trim the stems of the daisies to the desired length. Fill flower vials with water and insert a daisy in each vial.

Wrap tissue paper around each flower vial and place the vials in the container.

Gather

Assorted gerbera daisies

Plastic flower vials

Assorted tissue paper

Purchased box container

Refer to Glue Gun Safety Precautions on page 15 before beginning fast faux finish project.

fast faux finish

Choose silk flowers in an array of fun colors to create this joyous wreath. Trim flower stems, hot glue flowers and leaves to a grapevine wreath for a sunny summer decoration.

shell
shadow box

Relive your fondest summer memories by personalizing this purchased shadow box with some favorite photos, shells and sand.

1. Paint the outside surfaces of the wood frame blue. When the paint is dry, apply a coat of white. Use sandpaper to distress the frame by removing some of the white paint and allowing the blue to show through in places.

2. Cover the backboard with scrapbook paper and adhere with paper adhesive. Arrange and mount the photos on the paper, planning for the height of the sand and the mat opening. Hot glue shells and dried flowers around the pictures as desired.

3. To prevent the sand from seeping out, apply a thin line of hot glue on the inside of the frame along the bottom and lower side edges. Immediately place the glass in the frame and let the glue set. Insert the mat in the frame.

4. Pour sand into the bottom of the shadow box and add shells. Place the back on the shadow box. Seal the box with a bead of glue along the edges of the back; let the glue dry. Shake the box to arrange the sand and shells as desired.

Gather

Shadow box

Acrylic paint: blue and white

Paint brush

Sandpaper

Scrapbook papers

Paper adhesive

Photos (our photos were printed in sepia tones to blend with the colors of the shells)

Shells

Dried, bleached flowers

Hot glue gun and glue sticks

Craft sand

Refer to Glue Gun Safety Precautions on page 15 before beginning this project.

hydrangea
wreath

*P*ay tribute to summer's favorite flower, the hydrangea,
by designing a wreath in an array of its many beautiful colors.

1 Hold a hydrangea stem close to the wreath frame, weave the stem through the frame to achieve desired placement. Cut a length of florist's wire and wire the stem to the frame.

2 Place one or two hydrangea stems over the wired end of the first stem. Wire the stems to the frame.

3 Continue adding hydrangea stems in the same manner until the wreath frame is completely covered.

4 To attach the last stem, lift up the first and wire the last stem under it. Attach a wire to the wreath frame for hanging.

Gather

Wire wreath frame

Dried hydrangea stems

Florist's wire

Wire cutters

Refer to Glue Gun Safety Precautions on page 15 before beginning fast faux finish project.

fast faux finish

Use a twig wreath base and silk flowers for this heart-shaped wreath. Trim flower stems, then hot glue flowers and leaves to wreath for a quick door hanging.

seashell
wreath

Remember a special beach vacation with this unique wreath wrapped in netting and embellished with starfish, sand dollars, shells and a bit of greenery.

1 Hot glue one end of ribbon to the back of foam wreath. Wrap the ribbon around the wreath, slightly overlapping the edges to completely cover the foam. Glue the ribbon end to the back.

2 Cover the front of the wreath with fish netting. Hot glue cut edges of netting to the back of the wreath.

3 Beginning with the largest and progressing to the smallest, individually hot glue the seashells, starfish and sand dollars on the wreath. Hold each in place until the glue sets. Hot glue greenery to the wreath, tucking the ends under the shells.

Gather

Foam wreath with flat back and curved front

Cream ribbon
(1 1/2-inch-wide)

Hot glue gun
and glue sticks

Fish netting

Assorted seashells, starfish and sand dollars

Artificial greenery

Refer to Glue Gun Safety Precautions on page 15 before beginning this project.

fast faux finish

Pouring fine sand into a souvenir conch shell creates a clever display stand for a beach or ocean photo.

butterfly
shadow box

A butterfly composed of pastel painted skeleton leaves creates an illusion of floating when placed inside a purchased shadow box.

Remove the glass and backboard from the shadow box. Using the sponge brush, paint the outside surfaces of the shadow box purple. When the paint is dry, sand lightly and wipe off the dust with a clean cloth. Use a sponge brush to apply a coat of cream to the previously painted surfaces. Let dry. Use sandpaper to distress the shadow box, lightly sanding to remove some of the cream paint and allowing the purple to show through.

 Plan the position of the leaves for the butterfly and decide on colors. Use the sponge brush to paint the leaves the selected color, using a new paper plate for each color. Let the leaves dry.

 Hot glue the leaves together to create the butterfly, applying glue to the stems only. Let the glue set.

 Trim the stem from the lagurus just below the flower head. Add enough water to the container to cover the flower head. Color the water with the yellow food coloring and immerse the flower head. Remove the flower head when it is desired color and let dry. Hot glue the flower head in place on the leaves for the butterfly's body.

Cover the backboard with scrapbook paper and adhere with paper adhesive. Center the butterfly and hot glue onto scrapbook paper.

Shadow box

Acrylic paint: purple and cream and assorted colors for butterfly

Sponge brush (1-inch)

Sandpaper

Clean cloth

Two sizes of skeleton leaves

Paper plates

Hot glue gun and glue sticks

Dried lagurus (rabbit tail grass)

Yellow food coloring

Small plastic container

Scrapbook paper

Paper adhesive

Refer to Glue Gun Safety Precautions on page 15 before beginning this project.

fast faux finish

Add a touch of spring to your desk by gluing one of these butterflies to a paperweight.

beachcomber
stringer

Collect feathers, shells, stones and other items picked up along the beach or nature trail for this unusual decorative copper hanger.

1 Cut a 30-inch length of copper wire. Make a loop at one end of the wire for hanging. Use a needle nose pliers to twist the wire around itself.

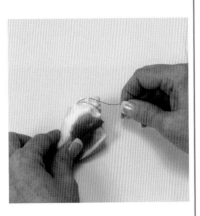

2 Arrange the objects in the desired order. Beginning at the top, attach the first object by wrapping the wire around it until secure. Be creative with the wire, wrapping it around the object as little or as much as you like or using openings in the objects.

22-Gauge copper wire

Wire cutters

Needle nose pliers

Assorted natural objects, such as beach glass, rocks, feathers, shells, twigs, bones, and glass beads

3 Continue adding the objects to the wire in this manner, leaving as much space between them as desired. Add additional wire when needed, wrapping the new length around the last object or twisting it onto the end of the original wire. Curl each wire end or twist it around itself.

gourd *hanger*

*E*mbellish a dried kettle gourd with artificial flowers for an interesting natural hanger that takes only minutes to complete.

1 Drill a hole through the neck of the gourd.

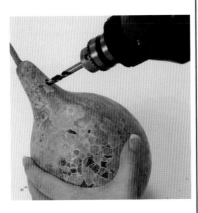

2 Break off the stem about 1/2-inch above the top of gourd. Spray paint the gourd if desired; let dry.

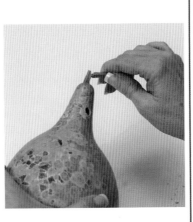

3 Thread the leather lace through the hole. Bring the ends of the leather lace together and knot about 3 inches from the ends for hanging.

4 Beginning with the largest flowers and progressing to the smallest, individually hot glue the flowers to the neck of the gourd. Hold each in place until the glue sets.

Gather

Dried kettle gourd, with long neck and stem

Drill

Acrylic crafter's spray paint

Assorted artificial flowers

Hot glue gun and glue sticks

Leather lace

Refer to Glue Gun Safety Precautions on page 15 before beginning this project.

fast faux finish

Turn a large kettle gourd into a vase by cutting it with a serrated knife, taking out the seeds, painting it and adding pebbles for stability.

wheat
centerpiece

*T*ie a length of sheer ribbon around graceful stalks of wheat to form a miniature sheaf for a fitting seasonal centerpiece surrounded by fresh flowers.

1 Hot glue sheet moss to completely cover plastic foam cone.

2 Wrap the rubber band several times around the cone 3 inches from the top.

3 Insert wheat shafts between the rubber band and the cone, using enough to completely cover the cone.

4 Tie ribbon into a large bow, covering the rubber band.

5 Center the wheat-covered cone on a large plate. Remove the stems from the flowers and arrange the flower heads around base of the cone.

Gather

Plastic foam cone
(10-inch-tall)

Sheet moss

Hot glue gun
and glue sticks

Rubber band

Multi-colored wheat shafts

Sheer ribbon
(2 1/2-inch-wide)

Large plate

Fresh flowers

*Refer to Glue Gun
Safety Precautions on page 15
before beginning this project.*

fast faux finish

Pick a pack of colorful peppers and add some leafy greens for a centerpiece to spice up your summer table.

autumn

naturals
gift bag

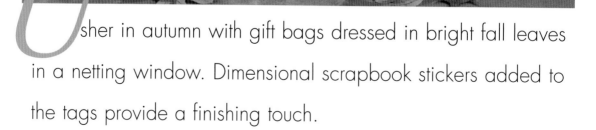

Usher in autumn with gift bags dressed in bright fall leaves in a netting window. Dimensional scrapbook stickers added to the tags provide a finishing touch.

 **1** Cut a frame from one color of card stock to fit on the front of the gift bag. Make the top of the frame wide enough to accommodate a dimensional sticker.

 2 Cut a piece of nylon netting slightly smaller than the outside dimensions of the frame. Position the netting on the bag front with the leaves behind the netting. Glue the edges of the netting to the bag; let the glue set. Glue the frame over the netting.

 3 Embellish the frame with 5/8"-wide strips cut from the second color of card stock, using a decorative-edge scissors for the inner edges. Add stickers to the frame.

 4 Tie fibers to the bag handle. Center additional stickers on several tags and attach the tags to the ends of some of the fibers. Wrap the gift with tissue paper and place in bag.

Gather

Purchased gift bag
with handles

2 Contrasting sheets
of card stock

Nylon netting

Dried leaves

Craft glue

Decorative-edge scissors

Dimensional
scrapbook stickers

Coordinating fibers

Scrapbook tags

Tissue paper

stone bracelets

String together assorted natural stone and glass beads in a combination of your favorite colors for fabulous jewelry to complement any wardrobe.

**String a crimp tube and one half of the toggle clasp on one end of the wire. Bring about 1" of wire back through the crimp tube. Use the crimping pliers to flatten and then fold the crimp tube in half.

 String the beads, spacers and charms on the wire in the desired order.

When the bracelet is the desired length, string a crimp tube and the second half of the toggle clasp onto the end of the wire. Bring the remaining end of the wire back through the crimp tube and several other beads. Using a needle nose pliers, pull on the wire end so the crimp tube is against the last bead and there is a small loop holding the clasp. Flatten and fold the crimp tube. Trim the excess wire with the wire snippers.

Add a bead dangle to one end of the toggle clasp if desired. Use two pliers to open the jump ring, moving the ends in opposite directions. Place the bead on the jump ring and then the jump ring on the clasp. Move the ends of the ring back together to close.

Assorted natural stone beads

Assorted glass beads

Assorted gold leaf charms

Assorted gold spacers

Gold toggle clasp

Flexible beading wire (12-inch piece)

2 Gold crimp tubes per bracelet

Crimping pliers

Needle nose pliers

Wire snippers

Gold jump ring (optional)

leaf&wheat
gift bow

Call attention to a special occasion by wrapping a gift with this impressive leaf and wheat bow. Finish the look with a decorative ribbon.

1 Spray the back of the leaves with paint, using a variety of colors on each. Let the paint dry.

2 Hot glue the stem ends of three leaves together, forming the base of the bow. Add a couple more leaves, adjusting their direction to fill in the areas between the first leaves.

3 Trim the wheat heads, leaving a short stem. Tuck the heads between the leaves and hot glue in place.

4 Make three loops with the ribbon and hot glue to the center of the leaves. Hot glue several wheat heads between the ribbon loops.

5 Wrap the package with paper and wire-edge ribbon. Hot glue the bow to the center top.

Gather

Large dried or purchased maple leaves

Acrylic crafter's spray paint in a variety of colors

Dried wheat

Fall patterned wire-edge ribbon (1 1/2-inch-wide)

Hot glue gun and glue sticks

Wrapping paper

Refer to Glue Gun Safety Precautions on page 15 before beginning this project.

fast faux finish

An ordinary recipe card becomes a special keepsake when embellished with seasonal stickers and grandma's secret pie recipe.

leaf
note cards

Deliver the feeling of autumn with note cards decorated with pressed leaves and flowers enhanced with pigments.

1 Plan the arrangement of pressed leaves and flowers on the card and envelope.

2 Dip the paintbrush in water, then in the pigment powder, and back in the water. Blot off excess moisture from the brush on a paper towel. Brush the powder onto the pressed leaves and flowers; let dry.

3 Beginning with the bottom pieces and working with one at a time, use the tip of a toothpick to apply a small amount of clear craft glue to the back of each piece. Carefully press each in place on the card and envelope. Let the glue dry.

4 To add ribbon, fold a length of ribbon in half and insert the fold through the hole from the back of the card, forming a loop. Thread the ribbon ends through the loop and pull on the ends, drawing the loop up against the top of the card.

Gather

Artist's paintbrushes

Small bowl of water

Perfect Pearls™ pigment kit

Paper towels

Pressed leaves and flowers

Purchased cards
with envelopes

Clear craft glue

Toothpicks

Ribbon (optional)

woodland
invitation

S et the mood for a special event by creating handwritten invitations tucked into a vellum pocket. Embellish the cards with autumn leaves and fibers.

 Cut a piece of handmade paper to fit the envelope for the base of the invitation. Layer two or three different papers centered on the base, each one slightly smaller than the last.

 Use the printed vellum to make an envelope for the right half of the invitation. Add a scrapbook sticker on the envelope and mount it on the invitation.

 Using word-print scrapbook paper that conveys your theme, tear the saying from the paper or write a saying on a scrap of paper. Attach the saying to the top left corner of the invitation. Add a dried leaf below the saying.

 Cut a handmade paper insert to fit the vellum envelope. Embellish the insert with scrapbook stickers. Make a small loop with fiber and attach to the back of the insert. Write event, date and time on insert and put in the vellum envelope.

Assorted handmade papers

Purchased envelope

Printed vellum
for attached envelope

Word-print scrapbook
paper (optional)

Dried leaf

Fibers

Craft glue

suede
napkin tie

*T*ouch-up your holiday table with a unique tie for your cloth napkins. Feathers and glass beads are attached to suede lacing for a festive fall look.

Cut two 5" lengths of beading wire. String a crimp bead and the top loop of a cord tip on one end of each wire. Bring approximately 1" of wire back through the crimp bead. Use the crimp pliers to secure the crimp bead.

 String beads on each wire as desired so the beaded areas measure 1 1/2" to 2".

 String a crimp bead and another cord tip onto each wire. Bring the wire end back through the crimp bead and several other beads. Using a needle nose pliers, pull on the wire end so the crimp bead is against the last bead and there is a small wire loop securing the cord tip. Crimp and trim the excess wire.

Make two small bunches of feathers. Let an end of one feather extend about 1/4" beyond the others in each bunch. Tightly wrap the feather ends together with brown floral tape.

 Insert each of the tape-wrapped feather ends into a cord tip. Be careful not to block the top loop. Gently close the sides of the cord tips with a flat nose pliers. Attach each of the remaining cord tips to an end of the lacing to complete the napkin tie.

 Wrap the napkin tie around a folded napkin and tie with an overhand knot.

Gather

Assorted beads

Feathers
(3 to 5-inches-long)

Brown floral tape

Suede lacing
(30-inch length)

4 Gold crimp beads

4 Cord tips

Beading wire

Wire snippers

Crimping pliers

Needle nose pliers

Flat nose pliers

fast faux finish

Add beads or stained glass charms to a purchased napkin ring. Just use a few dabs of hot glue to secure your embellishments.

Refer to Glue Gun Safety Precautions on page 15 before beginning this project.

feather
place mats

Charm dinner guests with festive place mats created with feather fronds and a circle of felt.

1 Cut a 6"-diameter circle from the center of a paper plate.

2 Trim the wire from each feather frond with wire cutters.

3 Hot glue the rounded end of a feather frond to the center of the paper circle. Hot glue the second frond to the circle to overlap the first. Continue gluing fronds around the plate in this manner until the paper circle is completely covered.

4 Cut a circle of brown felt large enough to cover the trimmed end of the fronds. Hot glue the felt circle in place.

Gather

Paper plate

Feather fronds
(8-10)

Wire cutters

Hot glue gun
and glue sticks

Brown felt

Wire cutters

*Refer to Glue Gun
Safety Precautions on page 15
before beginning this project.*

fast faux finish

Complete your fall table with a centerpiece that utilizes a feather place mat. Top the place mat with a bright colored plate filled with pears, leaves and acorns

feather
centerpiece

Combine dried grasses, flowers and other fall foliage to create this one-of-a-kind autumn centerpiece. A purchased grapevine wreath serves as the base.

1 Hot glue a variety of dried grasses to four evenly spaced areas on the top of the wreath.

2 Wrap the ribbon four times around the wreath so wraps fall between the grass areas. Hot glue the ribbon ends to the back.

3 Hot glue feather balls and seedpods in groups of 3-5 on each grass area. Attach each individually and hold in place until the glue sets.

4 Hot glue feathers, dried flowers and additional dried grasses to the wreath, tucking the ends underneath the feather balls and seedpods.

5 Position centerpiece on table and add a candle or other decorative item to the center opening.

Gather

Grapevine wreath
(14-inch-diameter)

Assorted dried grasses
and flowers

Sheer white ribbon
(5/8-inch wide)

Feather balls
(10-12)

Seedpods

Feathers

Hot glue gun
and glue sticks

*Refer to Glue Gun
Safety Precautions on page 15
before beginning this project.*

feather *party favor*

Company will flock to the table when they discover these adorable feather party favors. These plume-tailed birds are quick, easy to make and guests will love to take them home.

Cut the feather ball in half for the body. Use the direction of the feathers on the half-ball to determine the front and back of the body.

Hot glue the ends of assorted feathers together to create the tail. Hot glue the tail to the back of the body so the tail curves forward over the body.

Trim the pompom to make the fibers shorter and denser for the head. Hot glue the head to the front of the body about 1" from the cut edge. Add the glass beads for eyes. Cut a small triangle of tan felt for the beak and hot glue in place.

Cut a 3"-diameter circle of brown felt and glue to the bottom of the body.

Gather

Feather ball
(3-inch-diameter)

Assorted feathers

Brown furry pompom
(1—1 1/2-inch-diameter)

Glass beads (2)

Brown felt

Scrap of tan felt

Hot glue gun
and glue sticks

*Refer to Glue Gun
Safety Precautions on page 15
before beginning this project.*

dried naturals wreath

Welcome visitors to your home with an autumn wreath made from nature. Feathers and seedpods are arranged on a background of dried foliage.

 **1** Separate the Spanish moss into pieces. Hot glue a thin layer of moss to the entire front of the wreath, including the sides. It is not necessary to completely cover the grapevine.

 2 Hot glue sprigs of baby's breath to the front surface of the wreath. Add a sprinkling of dried flowers to the front surface.

 3 Visualize the wreath as a clock face and position groups of seedpods at 4 o'clock and between 9 and 10 o'clock on the front of the wreath. Do not attach.

 4 Select an assortment of dried flowers and grasses to embellish the seedpods. Trim the stems to the desired length. Add feathers to the dried assortments with the feathers pointing up on the right half of the wreath and down on the left half.

Hot glue the assortments in place so the ends will be covered by the seedpods. Individually hot glue the seedpods in place and hold until the glue sets.

 5 For hanger, position the ribbon at the center top of the wreath. Bring the ends together and knot the ribbon close to the wreath and then again near the ends.

Gather

Grapevine wreath
(18-inch-diameter)

Spanish moss

Baby's breath

Assorted dried flowers
and grasses

Seedpods

Long red feathers

Fall-patterned ribbon

Hot glue gun
and glue sticks

*Refer to Glue Gun
Safety Precautions on page 15
before beginning this project.*

bittersweet *gathering*

*W*arm tones of brown and orange contrast with brightly colored Japanese lanterns and bittersweet to create a festive door hanging.

 **1** Tie twigs into a bundle with twine or wire about 6" from the top, creating a loop for hanging.

2 Add broom corn and Japanese lanterns to the bunch. Decide if there is a front and back or if the hanging will be visible from all sides, such as on a glass door. Keep this in mind when adding flowers. When you're happy with the arrangement, secure with twine or wire.

 3 Knot raffia around the bunch to cover the wire.

 **4** Embellish with bittersweet, poking stems into the bundle.

Gather

Twigs

Dried Japanese lanterns and broom corn in 3 colors

Bittersweet

Multi-colored raffia

Twine or florist's wire

Wire cutters

eucalyptus *wreath*

*B*uild a fragrant hanging that beckons friends into your home. Two wreaths, twig and eucalyptus, team up with leaves and grasses in this seasonal decoration.

1 Visualize the eucalyptus wreath as a clock face and arrange a variety of silk leaves between 4 and 10 o'clock on the wreath. Hot glue the leaves in place.

2 Place the embellished eucalyptus wreath on the front surface of the twig wreath.

3 Turn the wreaths over, keeping the eucalyptus wreath centered on the twig wreath. Wire the wreaths together until secure.

Gather

Twig wreath

Eucalyptus wreath
to fit on twig wreath

Variety of silk
and natural leaves

Hot glue gun
and glue sticks

Florist's wire

Wire cutters

*Refer to Glue Gun
Safety Precautions on page 15
before beginning this project.*

gourmet gourds

Arrange gourds of varying textures, colors and shapes around a glass candleholder for a stunning centerpiece.

1 Sort the gourds by size and color.

2 Center the candleholder on the platter and place the largest gourds around the holder. Arrange the medium-sized gourds around the largest ones.

3 Position the smallest gourds over those already on the platter, filling in any open spaces. Add leaves, tucking some underneath the gourds.

4 To fill the candleholder, place bittersweet in it, leaving enough space for the candle. Fill the candleholder with water. Float candle on the water, checking to be sure the wick sits below the holder's rim.

Gather

Assorted gourds in a variety of sizes

Large platter or shallow bowl

Glass candleholder

Fall leaves

Bittersweet

Floating candle

mini gourd candleholders

Create an interesting grouping by turning gourds into candleholders. Embellish with glass beads for an elegant look.

1 Very carefully remove the stem area from the gourd. Check your progress often using a candle to determine the size of hole needed to accommodate candle. The candle should fit firmly and stand straight in the hole.

2 Cut small pieces from the glass bead stem with wire cutters. Hot glue the beads to the gourd, positioning them around the hole.

Gather

Mini pumpkin gourds

Craft knife or sharp kitchen knife

Taper candles (10-12-inch)

Assorted glass beads on stems

Wire cutters

Hot glue gun and glue sticks

Refer to Glue Gun Safety Precautions on page 15 before beginning this project.

fast faux finish

Fill a terra cotta container with colorful gourds and place in the center of a purchased grapevine wreath. Hot glue leaves and ribbon in fall colors for a quick centerpiece.

gourd
bird feeder

*T*reat your feathered friends to ears of corn and a buffet of seeds served from hollowed-out gourds. This special treat guarantees repeat visitors throughout the fall and winter.

1 Cut the gourds in half with a sharp knife. Use a spoon to remove the seeds. Fill the gourd halves with birdseed.

2 Lay the evergreen wreath on the ground under a tree or near a shrub. Garnish the wreath with seed sprigs. Arrange the filled gourd halves on the wreath. Place ears of corn in the center of the wreath.

3 Gourd halves can be secured to wreath if desired. Poke two holes through the bottom of the gourd half with an awl. Cut a length of wire and insert each of the wire ends through one of the holes from the cut side of the gourd. Use the wire ends to secure the gourd half to the wreath.

Gather

Assorted gourds

Spoon and sharp knife

Birdseed

Real or artificial evergreen wreath

Sprigs of wheat, oats or other bird-type seeds

Ears of corn

Awl, florist's wire, and wire cutters (optional)

sponge painted
gourds

Decorate a holiday tree or wreath with gourds that have been dried and painted in festive colors.

1 Wipe the gourds with a cloth to remove dust and dirt.

2 Use the natural sponge to dab small amounts of paint on the gourds, using as many colors as you like to completely cover the gourds with paint. Let dry.

3 Use the sponge again to highlight the gourds with metallic gold. Let dry.

4 Cut a 6-7" length of copper wire for each gourd. Make a small loop at the center of the wire. Center the loop on a twig and wrap the wire ends around it. Keep the wraps close together and trim the wire as desired. Hot glue the wire-wrapped twig near the base of the stem.

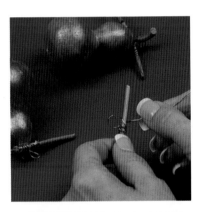

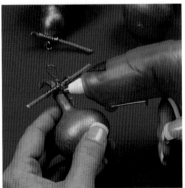

Gather

Assorted mini bottle gourds, dried and with stems

Clean, dry cloth

Acrylic paints in metallic gold and other desired colors

Small natural sponge

Light-gauge copper wire

Wire cutters

Pieces of twigs (2 1/2—3 1/2-inch)

Hot glue gun and glue sticks

Refer to Glue Gun Safety Precautions on page 15 before beginning this project.

pinecone
ornament

Crown a pine cone with small leaves and clusters of red berries.
Use holiday ribbon to hang the ornament in a favorite window.

1 Hot glue the stem of two silk leaves near the center bottom of the cone; the cone bottom is now the top of the ornament. Add a small cluster of berries to lie on the leaves. Attach dried red sprigs to fan out in all directions from the center top of the ornament.

2 Cut five 5" lengths of holiday ribbon. Fold each length in half and hot glue the ends to the center top of the ornament, forming the bow.

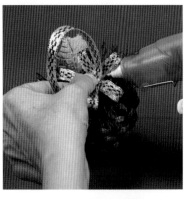

3 For the hanging loop, cut an 8" length of ribbon. Fold the ribbon in half and hot glue ends to the center of bow.

Pinecone
(approximately 3-inches tall)

2 Silk leaves

Artificial red berries

Dried red sprigs

Wire-edge holiday ribbon
(3/8-inch-wide)

Hot glue gun
and glue sticks

*Refer to Glue Gun
Safety Precautions on page 15
before beginning this project.*

mini pinecone snowglobe

Fill a glass ornament with sequins and mini pinecones and set atop a painted terra cotta pot. This simple snowglobe makes a perfect party favor.

1 Using the sponge brush, paint all surfaces of the terra cotta pot white. When the paint is dry, hot glue a length of ribbon around the rim of the pot. Add snowflake stickers to the front.

2 Remove the metal cap from the clear glass ornament. Make a mixture of mini pinecones, snowflake sequins and artificial snowflakes. Carefully spoon the mixture through the opening, filling the ornament about 1/4 full. Pinecones and sequins may need to be gently pushed through the opening.

3 Hot glue metal cap on ornament. Place the ornament upside down on the pot to complete the snow globe.

Gather

Terra cotta pot
(2 1/2-inch tall)

White acrylic paint

Sponge brush

Blue ribbon
(5/8-inch-wide)

Adhesive snowflake
stickers

Clear glass ball ornament
(2 1/2-inch-diameter)

Mini pinecones

Snowflake sequins

Artificial snowflakes

Hot glue gun
and glue sticks

*Refer to Glue Gun
Safety Precautions on page 15
before beginning this project.*

hydrangea garland

Be ready for a host of compliments when holiday company notices this beautiful garland, artfully enhanced with hydrangea, evergreen and flower heads, on your fireplace mantel.

1 If using fresh evergreen, place cotton batting or a cloth on the mantle before beginning. Lay evergreen garland on the mantle, shaping the branches as desired.

2 Trim stems from hydrangea and lay the flower heads evenly spaced on the garland, alternating the colors as desired. Trim clusters of flowers, berries and beads from the assorted stems. Tuck the cut ends of the cluster underneath the flower heads.

3 Make a multi-loop bow with the sheer ribbon, adding small clusters of the assorted stems to the center of the bow if desired. Secure the bow to one end of the garland.

Gather

Fresh or artificial evergreen garland

Dried or artificial hydrangea in several colors

Assorted flower, berry and bead stems

Wire-edge sheer ribbon (2 1/2-inch-wide)

Fine wire

Wire cutters

lunaria
centerpiece

Sparkling fruit, glass beads and lunaria adorn evergreen sprigs tucked into a purchased wire wreath. A decorative candle and holder complete this simple arrangement.

 Tuck the ends of the evergreen sprigs into the wire wreath frame.

 Arrange the sparkled fruit on the evergreen sprigs. Cut pieces from the lunaria and sparkled sprigs. Tuck the cut ends of the pieces into the evergreen.

Position centerpiece on table and place a candleholder in the center opening.

Wire wreath frame

Fresh evergreen sprigs

Assorted sparkled fruits

Dried or artificial lunaria (money-plant)

Sparkled sprigs

Candleholder and candle

feather
stocking

*A*dorn a purchased stocking with feathers and beaded fringe for a shimmering holiday decoration.

1 Cut the beaded fringe into individual strands. Space the beaded strands evenly along the bottom of the stocking and sew.

2 Hot glue the feather boa to the bottom edge of the stocking cuff. Sew the ornament or pin the brooch to the cuff.

3 Fold the ribbon in half and sew the ends to the inside top corner of the stocking on the heel side. This will be the hanging loop. Arrange fresh greens and sparkled sprigs in the stocking.

Gather

Purchased stocking with fur cuff

Purchased beaded fringe

Feather boa

Jeweled ornament or costume brooch

Ribbon (12-inch-length)

Fresh greens

Sparkled sprigs

Needle and thread

Hot glue gun and glue sticks

Refer to Glue Gun Safety Precautions on page 15 before beginning this project.

fast faux finish

A sheer butterfly added to the outside of a tall candleholder sets the stage for a cozy evening.

greens
wreath

Trim the front door with an interesting wreath of
evergreen and white berry sprigs. Mix in glass ornaments
for a holiday welcome.

1 Fill the wire wreath with evergreen sprigs.

2 Hot glue glass ball ornaments evenly spaced on the front surface of the wreath. Add clusters of red berries near each of the ornaments.

3 Trim the white berry sprigs to the desired length. Insert the cut ends of the sprigs into the wreath and hot glue in place.

4 For hanger, cut a length of ribbon. Weave the ribbon through the center top of the wreath. Bring the ribbon ends together and knot.

Gather

Wire wreath

Artificial evergreen sprigs

White glass ball ornaments

Artificial red berries

White berry sprigs

Hot glue gun and glue sticks

Wire-edge holiday ribbon
(2 1/2-inch-wide)

*Refer to Glue Gun
Safety Precautions on page 15
before beginning this project.*

fast faux finish

A candy cane lined bowl filled with chocolate candies displays your great taste.

holly gift basket

Warm up a purchased basket with greenery and ribbon, then fill with small presents or candies for a gift that's twice as nice.

1. Line basket with green tissue paper. Press it firmly to the sides of the basket.

2. Cut pieces of fresh greenery and use to line the basket. Insert greenery between the tissue paper and the basket sides. Place gifts inside the basket.

3. Make a multi-loop bow with the ribbon. Insert sprigs of greenery, holly leaves and berries into the center of the bow. Wire the bow to the handle of the basket.

Gather

Wire basket

Green tissue paper

Flat fresh greenery

Holiday ribbon
(2 1/2-inch-wide)

Florist's wire

Wire cutters

Holly leaves and berries

fast faux finish

Tuck a handmade, personalized gift card into a basket. Card stock and scrapbook stickers make it easy to create.

evergreen *tins*

Decorate antique-looking tins with adhesive holiday scrapbook designs. Complete the seasonal look by filling the tins with fresh greenery and holly leaves and berries.

1 Plan the placement of the scrapbook designs on the front of the tin container.

2 Press scrapbook designs in place.

3 Fill the containers with fresh greens, holly leaves and berries.

Tin containers
with handles

Adhesive scrapbook
designs

Fresh greens

Holly leaves and berries